Morning, Noon, and Night

POEMS TO FILL YOUR DAY

● ● ● ● ● ● ● ● ● ● ● ● ● ● ● ● ● ● ● ●

SELECTED BY **Sharon Taberski**

ILLUSTRATED BY **Nancy Doniger**

MONDO

To my children, Ann, Matt, and Dan. S.T.

To Arlene, Jerry, and Andy, with love,
and to my son Cody, who has taught me joy. N.D.

ACKNOWLEDGMENTS

Atheneum Books for "Shadows." Reprinted with the permission of Atheneum Books for Young Readers, an imprint of Simon & Schuster Children's Publishing Division from CATCH ME A WIND by Patricia Hubbell. Copyright © 1968 by Patricia Hubbell.

Bantam Books for "I'm Going to Say I'm Sorry" from THE OTHER SIDE OF THE DOOR by Jeff Moss. Copyright © 1991 by Jeff Moss. Used by permission of Bantam Books, a division of Bantam Doubleday Dell Publishing Group, Inc.

Jane Baskwill for "Has Anybody Seen My Things?" from PASS THE POEMS PLEASE. Used with permission of the author.

Boyds Mills Press, Inc. for "My Book!" from SOMEBODY CATCH MY HOMEWORK by David L. Harrison. Published by Wordsong, Boyds Mills Press, Inc. Reprinted by permission.

Dutton Signet for "Me" from ME by Inez Hogan. Copyright 1954 by Inez Hogan, Copyright © renewed 1983 by Frank Hogan. Used by permission of Dutton Signet, a division of Penguin Books USA Inc.

Aileen Fisher for "After a Bath" from UP THE WINDY HILL by Aileen Fisher. Used with permission of the author.

HarperCollins Publishers for "Pencils" from WHO SHRANK MY GRANDMOTHER'S HOUSE? POEMS OF DISCOVERY by Barbara Juster Esbensen. Copyright © 1992 by Barbara Juster Esbensen. Selection reprinted by permission of HarperCollins Publishers.

Henry Holt and Co., Inc. for "Shoelaces" from IS SOMEWHERE ALWAYS FAR AWAY? by Leland B. Jacobs. Copyright © 1993 by Allan D. Jacobs. Reprinted by permission of Henry Holt and Co., Inc.

Bobbi Katz for "Cat Kisses." Copyright © 1974 by Bobbi Katz. Used with permission of the author.

Alfred A. Knopf, Inc. for "Poem" from THE DREAM KEEPER AND OTHER POEMS by Langston Hughes. Copyright 1932 by Alfred A. Knopf, Inc. and renewed 1960 by Langston Hughes. Reprinted by permission of the publisher.

Little, Brown and Company for "Pick Up Your Room" from FATHERS, MOTHERS, SISTERS, BROTHERS: A COLLECTION OF FAMILY POEMS by Mary Ann Hoberman. Copyright © 1991 by Mary Ann Hoberman. "Sweet Dreams" from CUSTARD AND COMPANY by Ogden Nash. Copyright © 1961, 1962 by Ogden Nash. Both by permission of Little, Brown and Company.

Marci Ridlon McGill for "Hamsters" from THAT WAS SUMMER by Marci Ridlon. Copyright © 1969 by Marci Ridlon. Published by Follett Publishing Co. Reprinted by permission of Marci Ridlon McGill.

G. P. Putnam's Sons for "Bursting" by Dorothy Aldis. Reprinted by permission of G. P. Putnam's Sons from ALL TOGETHER by Dorothy Aldis, copyright 1952 by Dorothy Aldis, © renewed 1980 by Roy E. Porter. "Going to Sleep" by Dorothy Aldis. Reprinted by permission of G. P. Putnam's Sons from HOP, SKIP AND JUMP! by Dorothy Aldis, copyright 1934, © renewed 1961 by Dorothy Aldis. "Kick a Little Stone" by Dorothy Aldis. Reprinted by permission of G. P. Putnam's Sons from BEFORE THINGS HAPPEN by Dorothy Aldis, copyright 1939 by Dorothy Aldis, © renewed 1967 by Mary Cornelia Aldis Porter.

Marian Reiner for "Morning" from WHISPERS AND OTHER POEMS by Myra Cohn Livingston. © 1958, 1986 by Myra Cohn Livingston. "Sometimes" from I FEEL THE SAME WAY by Lilian Moore. Copyright © 1967 by Lilian Moore. "The Tree on the Corner" from I THOUGHT I HEARD THE CITY by Lilian Moore. Copyright © 1969 by Lilian Moore. "Wide Awake" from WIDE AWAKE AND OTHER POEMS by Myra Cohn Livingston. © 1959 by Myra Cohn Livingston. Copyright © Renewed 1987 Myra Cohn Livingston. "Writing on the Chalkboard" by Isabel Joshlin Glaser. Copyright © 1987 by Isabel Joshlin Glaser. All reprinted by permission of Marian Reiner for the authors.

Elizabeth Roach for "Crayons" from RHYMES ABOUT US by Marchette Chute. Published 1974 by E. P. Dutton. Copyright 1974 by Marchette Chute. Reprinted by permission of Elizabeth Roach.

Lois Simmie for "Bug" from AN ARMADILLO IS NOT A PILLOW by Lois Simmie, © 1986, published by Douglas & McIntyre. Reprinted by permission.

Simon & Schuster Inc. for "School Mornings." Reprinted with the permission of Simon & Schuster Books for Young Readers, an imprint of Simon & Schuster Children's Publishing Division from SECRETS OF A SMALL BROTHER by Richard J. Margolis. Copyright © 1984 Richard T. Margolis. "You're an Author Now." Reprinted with the permission of Simon & Schuster Books for Young Readers, an imprint of Simon & Schuster Children's Publishing Division from MRS. COLE ON AN ONION ROLL AND OTHER SCHOOL POEMS by Kalli Dakos. Text copyright © 1995 Kalli Dakos.

Scott Treimel for "A House" from ALL THAT SUNLIGHT. Copyright © 1967 by Charlotte Zolotow. Reprinted by permission of Scott Treimel New York on behalf of the Author.

Valerie Worth for "Lunchbox." Copyright 1992 by Valerie Worth. Used by permission.

Every effort has been made to trace the ownership of all copyrighted materials in this book and to obtain permission for their use.

Printed in Hong Kong by South China Printing Co. (1988) Ltd.
96 97 98 99 00 01   9 8 7 6 5 4 3 2 1

Designed by Sylvia Frezzolini Severance. Production by Our House.

The illustrations for this book were cut from colored papers and then painted with watercolor and gouache.

Library of Congress Cataloging-in-Publication Data
Morning, noon, and night : poems to fill your day / selected by Sharon Taberski;
illustrated by Nancy Doniger.
    p. cm.
    Summary: A selection of poems about the activities in a child's day,
written by poets including Myra Cohn Livingston, Jeff Moss, Langston Hughes,
and Charlotte Zolotow.
    ISBN 1-57255-128-3 (alk. paper). — ISBN 1-57255-127-5 (pbk. : alk. paper)
    1. Children's poetry, American. [1. American poetry—Collections.]
I. Taberski, Sharon. II. Doniger, Nancy, ill.
PS586.3.M68   1996
811.008'09282—dc20   95-25527
                                                          CIP
                                                          AC

CONTENTS

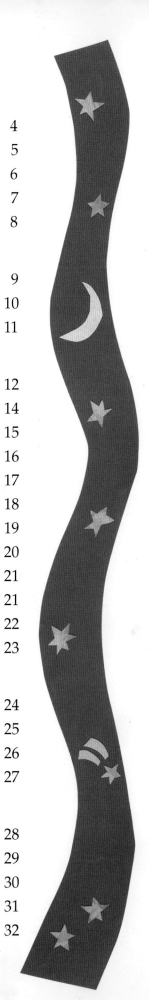

Waking Up

Cat Kisses   *Bobbi Katz*   4

Wide Awake   *Myra Cohn Livingston*   5

School Mornings   *Richard J. Margolis*   6

Morning   *Myra Cohn Livingston*   7

Has Anybody Seen My Things?   *Jane Baskwill*   8

On the Way to School

Shadows   *Patricia Hubbell*   9

Kick a Little Stone   *Dorothy Aldis*   10

The Tree on the Corner   *Lilian Moore*   11

During the School Day

My Book!   *David L. Harrison*   12

Writing on the Chalkboard   *Isabel Joshlin Glaser*   14

You're An Author Now   *Kalli Dakos*   15

Pencils   *Barbara Juster Esbensen*   16

Crayons   *Marchette Chute*   17

Hamsters   *Marci Ridlon*   18

Bug   *Lois Simmie*   19

Lunchbox   *Valerie Worth*   20

Through the Teeth   *Folk Rhyme*   21

Bursting   *Dorothy Aldis*   21

I'm Going to Say I'm Sorry   *Jeff Moss*   22

Poem   *Langston Hughes*   23

After School

Sometimes   *Lilian Moore*   24

Shoelaces   *Leland B. Jacobs*   25

A House   *Charlotte Zolotow*   26

Pick Up Your Room   *Mary Ann Hoberman*   27

Going to Bed

After a Bath   *Aileen Fisher*   28

Me   *Inez Hogan*   29

Going to Sleep   *Dorothy Aldis*   30

Night, Knight   *Anonymous*   31

Sweet Dreams   *Ogden Nash*   32

Cat Kisses

Sandpaper kisses
on a cheek or a chin—
that is the way
for a day to begin!

Sandpaper kisses—
a cuddle, a purr.
I have an alarm clock
that's covered with fur.

Bobbi Katz

Wide Awake

I have to jump
    out of bed
    and stretch my hands
    and rub my head,
    and curl my toes
    and yawn
    and shake
    myself
    all wide-awake!

Myra Cohn Livingston

School Mornings

On school days he gets up first.
The lamp glares.
The floor groans.
The faucet spits.
The hangers in our closet clang.
When my bed shakes,
I know he is tying his shoe.
Time to get up.

Richard J. Margolis

Morning

Everyone is tight asleep,
I think I'll sing a tune,
And if I sing it loud enough
I'll wake up someone – soon!

Myra Cohn Livingston

Has Anybody Seen My Things?

Has anybody seen my sock?
Or what about my shoe?
Has anybody seen my hat?
The one that's just brand new?
Has anybody seen my book?
Or what about my bear?
I have a place for all my things—
I just can't remember where!

Jane Baskwill

Shadows

Chunks of night
Melt
In the morning sun.
One lonely one
Grows legs
And follows me
To school.

Patricia Hubbell

Kick a Little Stone

When you are walking by yourself
Here's something nice to do:
Kick a little stone and watch it
Hop ahead of you.

The little stone is round and white,
It's shadow round and blue.
Along the sidewalk over the cracks
The shadow bounces too.

Dorothy Aldis

The Tree on the Corner

I've seen
the tree on the corner
in spring bud
and summer green.
Yesterday
it was yellow gold.

Then a cold
wind began to blow.
Now I know—
you really do not see
a tree
until you see
its bones.

Lilian Moore

My Book!

I did it!
I did it!
Come and look
At what I've done!
I read a book!
When someone wrote it
Long ago
For me to read,
How did he know
That this was the book
I'd take from the shelf
And lie on the floor
And read by myself?

I really read it!
Just like that!
Word by word,
From first to last!
I'm sleeping with
This book in bed,
This first FIRST book
I've ever read!

David L. Harrison

Writing on the Chalkboard

Up and down, my chalk goes.
– – – – – *Squeak, squeak, squeak!*
Hush, chalk.
Don't squawk.
Talk *softly* when you speak.

Isabel Joshlin Glaser

14

You're an Author Now

I'm writing,
I'm writing,
I'm writing in my book.
I'm writing,
I'm writing,
Oh, Teacher, come and look.

You're writing,
You're writing,
I'm glad you've learned how.
You're writing,
You're writing,
You're an author now.

Kalli Dakos

Pencils

Every word in your
pencil
is fearless   Ready to walk
the blue tightrope lines
Ready
to teeter and smile
down   Ready to come right out
and show you
thinking!

Barbara Juster Esbensen

Crayons

I've colored a picture with crayons.
    I'm not very pleased with the sun.
I'd like it much stronger and brighter
    And more like the actual one.
I've tried with the crayon that's yellow.
    I've tried with the crayon that's red.
But none of it looks like the sunlight
    I carry around in my head.

Marchette Chute

Hamsters

Hamsters are the nicest things
That anyone could own.
I like them even better than
Some dogs that I have known.

Their fur is soft, their faces nice.
They're small when they are grown.
And they sit inside your pocket
When you are all alone.

Marci Ridlon

Bug

In the window of the washroom
At our school yesterday,
A little bug was crawling
In its little buggy way.

I whispered in its tiny ear
To not make any noise;
Because it was a ladybug
And the washroom is for boys.

Lois Simmie

Lunchbox

They always
End up
Fighting—

The soft
Square
Sandwich,

The round
Heavy
Apple.

Valerie Worth

Through the Teeth

Through the teeth
And past the gums
Look out stomach,
Here it comes!

Folk Rhyme

Bursting

We've laughed until my cheeks are tight.
We've laughed until my stomach's sore.
If we could only stop we might
Remember what we're laughing for.

Dorothy Aldis

I'm Going to Say I'm Sorry

I'm going to say I'm sorry.
It's time for this quarrel to end.
I know that we both didn't mean it
and each of us misses a friend.
It isn't much fun being angry
and arguing's just the worst,
so I'm going to say I'm sorry . . .
just as soon as you say it first!

Jeff Moss

Poem

I loved my friend.
He went away from me.
There's nothing more to say.
The poem ends,
Soft as it began –
I loved my friend.

Langston Hughes

Sometimes

Sometimes
when I skip or hop
or when I'm
    jumping

Suddenly
I like to stop
and listen to me
    thumping.

Lilian Moore

Shoelaces

Although I've tried and
   tried and tried,
I cannot keep my laces
   tied.
I really don't know what to
   do–
Unless I stick them
   tied with glue–
Except that such a
   sticky mess
Would not be good for
   shoes, I guess.

Leland B. Jacobs

A House

Everyone has a house,
              a house,
everyone has a house.
The bear has a cave,
the bird a nest,
the mole a hole,
but what is best
is a house like ours
              with windows and doors
                and rugs and floors.
Everyone has a house,
              a house,
everyone has a house.

Charlotte Zolotow

Pick Up Your Room

Pick up your room, my mother says
    (She says it every day);
My room's too heavy to pick up
    (That's what I always say).

Drink up your milk, she says to me,
    Don't bubble like a clown;
Of course she knows I'll answer that
    I'd rather drink it down.

And when she says at eight o'clock,
    You must go right to bed,
We both repeat my answer:
    Why not go left instead?

Mary Ann Hoberman

After a Bath

After my bath
I try, try, try
to wipe myself
till I'm dry, dry, dry.

Hands to wipe
and fingers and toes
and two wet legs
and a shiny nose.

Just think how much
less time I'd take
if I were a dog
and could shake, shake, shake.

Aileen Fisher

Me

Sing to me—
Read to me—
Play with me, too.
Tell me you love me
Because I love you.

When you tuck me in bed
Don't turn out the light—
First tell me a story,
And kiss me, good night.

Inez Hogan

Going to Sleep

The safest feeling
In the world
Is to be lying
Warm and curled
In bed while in
The room next door
They talk; and then
Don't any more. . . .

Dorothy Aldis

Night, Knight

"Night, night,"
said one knight
to the other knight
the other night.
"Night, night, knight."

Anonymous

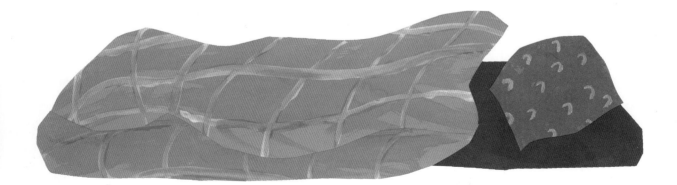

Sweet Dreams

I wonder as into bed I creep
What it feels like to fall asleep.
I've told myself stories, I've counted sheep,
But I'm always asleep when I fall asleep.
Tonight my eyes I will open keep,
And I'll stay awake till I fall asleep,
Then I'll know what it feels like to fall asleep,
Asleep,
Asleep,
Asleeep . . .

Ogden Nash